ENTER THE PROMISED LAND

–

The U.S. African American Restoration Act

Proposed Legislation To Establish Massive Federal Educational
Entitlements for African-Americans
and
A Collection of Photographs of African American Slavery
from the collections of the U.S. Library Of Congress

By

ISAIAS GAMBOA

All Proceeds from the sale of this publication will go towards passing
THE US AFRICAN AMERICAN RESTORATION ACT

For more information go to:

www.WeShallOvercomeFoundation.Org/RestorationAct

ENTER THE PROMISED LAND

The U.S. African American Restoration Act

Proposed Legislation to Establish Massive Federal Educational Entitlements for African-Americans

ISBN:1542477522
ISBN-13: 978-1542477529

All Proceeds from the sale of this book will go towards passing the US African American Restoration Act.

DEDICATION

In the name of God, this publication is humbly dedicated to the memory and legacy of kidnapped Africans, who were enslaved in the United States of America. —A proud people who prayed to God for freedom, justice and equality. In answer to their prayers and those of their descendants and in honor and remembrance of the blood, sweat, tears and lives they shed to build this country, The U.S. African American Restoration Act will provide for and ensure the everlasting peace and prosperity of their worthy descendants.

All Proceeds from the sale of this publication will go towards passing this historic legislation.

CONTENTS

INTRODUCTION

As did the Hebrews of Egypt, enslaved Africans in America once prayed to God for righteousness and emancipation from the cruel inhumanity of slavery. That prayer was answered through the passage of the "Emancipation Proclamation"—an executive order issued by President Abraham Lincoln on January 1, 1863. 100 years later, on August 28, 1963, the Rev. Dr. Martin Luther King Jr. stood on the steps of the Lincoln Memorial in Washington D.C. and declared; **"one hundred years later, the Negro is still not free".** That historic afternoon before a crowd of 250,000, the African American hymn, "We Shall Overcome" was sung at the beginning *and* end of Dr. King's historic, "I Have A Dream" speech. That hymn and speech were powerful vessels of truth, faith and hope. Forged from the prayers of the suffering and compassionate, these sacred proclamations carried the promise made to American Blacks by God that they would indeed "Overcome Someday".

More than fifty years later, African Americans cry, "Black Lives Matter!" Their tear-filled, blood-drenched cries for freedom, justice and equality once again appeal to the heavens to end the suffering, anguish, misery and torment they continue to suffer in America. No matter the pain, their spirits are not broken. No matter the cruelty, humiliation and indignity they must endure, they continue to pray to God. –And God is listening.

African Americans are not a broken people in need of repair; they are a distressed, oppressed and suffering people in need of restoration and restitution. Like any successful culture or civilization, in order to survive and prosper, American Blacks must rebuild their lives and futures on a deeply embedded foundation of high-quality education. –A freedom that has been legally, institutionally and categorically denied American Blacks for 400 years.

Experts the world over agree that education is the only proven solution to permanently eradicating poverty and crime. It is also the key to the cultural, economic, social and political transformation of Blacks in America.

The devastating generational byproducts of slavery in America and across the globe are well documented and have resulted in crippling emotional and psychological damage to the descendants of those once thriving Africans, who were kidnapped and enslaved for profit. The after-effects of slavery in America have also now manifested themselves into cancerous racial polarization and profound damage to the overall psychological and ideological state of the union. Among other effects, the malignant vestiges of Slavery, Jim Crow Laws, Mass

Incarceration, Redlining and other forms of Institutional Racism in the U.S. have metastasized into the five-to-one ratio of Black men incarcerated in America over that of Caucasian men (According the US Bureau of Justice Statistics). Although countless studies have demonstrated that African Americans do not commit more crimes than other Americans, due to institutionalized racial profiling by police, they are arrested and incarcerated in far greater numbers than non-African Americans. The disproportionate, mass incarcerations of Blacks have decimated families and continue to damage the lives and futures of African Americans long after slavery was abolished.

One would think that these empirical facts would be sufficient to cause positive changes in American domestic policy. Disturbingly however, in a 2014 study published in the journal, "Psychological Science", Stanford University psychology researchers, Rebecca Hetey and Jennifer Eberhardt found that "**White participants who were exposed to higher racial disparities in incarceration rates reported being more afraid of crime and more likely to support the kinds of punitive policies that exacerbate these racial disparities.**" In other words, presenting studies and statistics proving that African Americans have always and are still suffering hatred, discrimination and abuse because of the color of their skin, does not solve the problem for Blacks in America. In fact, it actually makes it worse. Instead of demonstrating outrage and compassion after being informed that Blacks are unjustly locked up five times as often as Whites, Americans clutch their purses tighter, put more locks on their doors and support harsher punishment of Blacks than Whites.

Perhaps this explains why, Detroit Congressman John Conyers' "Reparations Bill" - **"H.R.40 - Commission to Study Reparation Proposals for African-Americans Act",** after more than 28 years since he first proposed it, has not been dignified with so much as a congressional vote...let alone passed. The "HR 40" bill did not itself seek monetary reparations for American Blacks, but simply to secure a budget to establish a commission, which would then examine the institution and impact of slavery on American Blacks and recommend appropriate remedies. As we now know however, in America, demonstrating statistics on the negative health consequences of Blacks being lynched, increases rope sales.

Ironically, it is perhaps the newly elected Republican, President Donald J. Trump's own words—a man who has publicly discriminated against blacks all of his life, that best reveal the contempt with which far too many Americans still hold Blacks. In a rather disingenuous attempt to woo African American voters during his 2016 presidential campaign, Trump famously stated:

"What do you have to lose by trying something new like Trump? What do you have to lose? You live in your poverty, your schools are no good, you have no jobs, 58 percent of your youth is unemployed. What the hell do you have to lose?" In a 2015 Washington Post, investigative journalist Emily Badger wrote; *"The poverty that poor African Americans experience is often different from the poverty of poor whites. It's more isolating and concentrated. It extends out the door of a family's home and occupies the entire neighborhood around it, touching the streets, the schools, the grocery stores.*

"A poor black family, in short, is much more likely than a poor white one to live in a neighborhood where many other families are poor, too, creating what sociologists call the "double burden" of poverty. The difference is stark in most major metropolitan areas, according to recent data analyzed by Rutgers University's Paul Jargowsky in a new report for the Century Foundation... Concentrated poverty is getting worse because poor people — especially poor African Americans — are increasingly left behind. And a number of forces drive this pattern, including systematic discrimination, policies that have historically concentrated public housing and modern zoning laws that keep the poor out of wealthier communities"

Apparently unimpressed by Trump's heart-felt speech, 92 percent of African Americans voted *against* him in the 2016 Presidential election. Nonetheless, as we know, Donald J. Trump was elected the 45th President of the United States. As Rev. Dr. Martin Luther King put it: **"We must come to see that the roots of racism are very deep in our country, and there must be something positive and massive in order to get rid of all the effects of racism and the tragedies of racial injustice."** Dr. King was right. We know that, while critically important, studies alone wont solve the enduring trials and tribulations of American Blacks. In many cases, they may make things worse. However, there is good news. There *is* a solution.

AMERICA'S ADMISSION OF GUILT

In 2009, six months following the election of President Barack Obama, Iowa Senator Tom Harkin—a White man—successfully sponsored a bill, which admitted to the evils of slavery and apologized to Blacks on behalf of America. In presenting this bill to Congress, Senator Harkin stated the following:

"While the reconstruction amendments, the 13th amendment banning slavery, the 14th amendment granting full citizenship to all slaves, and the 15th amendment guaranteeing the right to vote supposedly signaled equality for all, widespread oppression continued. Jim Crow laws, African-Americans were denied voting rights, denied employment opportunities, denied access to public accommodations, denied entry into military service, denied criminal justice protections, denied housing, denied education, denied police protection, denied due process. In short, denied their very humanity.

"Not until the passage of the Civil Rights Act of 1964 and the Voting Rights Act of 1965 and other federal protections did legal -- legal -- segregation effectively cease in this country. The destructive effects of both slavery and Jim Crow remain, however. As President Bush noted, 'the racial bigotry did not end with slavery.' President Clinton stated that the racial divide is

'America's constant curse.' Today many African-Americans remained mired in poverty. Average incomes remain below that of white Americans. There remains an achievement gap in education and, for many, health conditions. African-Americans bear a disproportionate burden of disease and injury and death and disability. African- Americans are more over disproportionately involved with the criminal justice system in our prisons."

ENTITLEMENT

As a meaningful and long overdue gesture of atonement and contrition for what the New York Times has called, "America's Original Sin", I propose that the United States Congress pass, the **"U.S. AFRICAN AMERICAN RESTORATION ACT"** (USAARA).

Once passed, the USAARA will, without prejudice, provide to African Americans, regardless of economic status or criminal background, FULL post-secondary and vocational scholarship vouchers for tuition, books, materials, housing and meals. No direct cash disbursements need be made to any USAARA recipient.

So, who will pay to execute this LAW, they ask?

The answer is; it has *already* been paid for. –Paid for with the blood, sweat, tears and very lives of Africans, enslaved in America and whose unpaid forced labor was used to establish America's foundation and build it into what it is today. The value of that toil added to the cost of the murder, rape, torture, and abuse levied against African American slaves is indeed immeasurable. As such, the descendants of African American slaves will now be the direct beneficiaries of this historic and just entitlement. America will, once and for all, pay its moral debt to American Blacks.

How much will this cost, they ask?

Well, have you ever asked yourself that question when you see the police putting an African American youth into a patrol car? Consider that according to a recent College Board report, for the 2015/16 academic years, the average overall cost for tuition, fees, room and board to attend an in-state public college in America was $20,090. By comparison, according to the US Bureau of Justice Statistics, the average annual taxpayer cost in America of housing a prisoner is $31,286 per inmate with some states such as New York, as high as, $60,000 per prison inmate.

In addition, countless studies have concluded that education drastically reduces crime, recidivism and poverty rates. In other words, this historic legislation will, among other things, actually *save* U.S. taxpayers billions of dollars annually by providing African Americans with the educational resources they need to truly overcome—not just get by. –Resources, which have been historically and legally denied to them since first stepping—foot and shackle—onto American soil. These essential entitlements will also free American Blacks from generational and systemic cycles of educational, economic and parental poverty., which are essential to restoring all African Americans to their pre-slavery place of cultural stability, relevance, productivity, prosperity and self-sustainability. –These traits—the building blocks of any successful civilization, were systematically stripped from American Blacks through slavery and denied them through the legalized murder, hatred, racism and discrimination of Jim Crow Laws and institutional racism.

To be certain, the U.S. African American Restoration Act shall by no means constitute a "free lunch" for anyone. To begin with, the word, "Free" is unsuitable to describe these educational dispensations. As previously mentioned, a quality education for all African Americans must be considered an entitlement, which has been PAID IN FULL by the blood, sweat, tears and lives of their enslaved ancestors. That said, this program will mandate a full and sustained scholastic commitment from each and every recipient, in order to redeem USAARA educational vouchers. –Recipients must attend class and get passing grades in order for the federal funds to be disbursed to his or her chosen academic institution.

CONCLUSION

There is no downside here. This action is long overdue and in order to succeed MUST be supported by Americans of all races. We now ask for your support—as Americans—to stand with us and use any and all non-violent, legal means necessary to compel a bi-partisan congressional coalition as elected and paid servants of the American people, to sponsor and sign the U.S. AFRICAN AMERICAN RESTORATION ACT into federal law. In doing so, America will have finally atoned for its atrocities and close one of the darkest of chapters in its history. In doing so, America will truly earn the right to represent itself as, **"the land of the free and the home of the brave".**

For African Americans, education is and has always been the key to the gates of the "Promised Land". There can be no further obstacles standing in the way of the fulfillment of this dream.

In the words of Rev. Dr. Martin Luther King Jr.,

The Negro has no room to make any substantial compromises because his store of advantages is too small. He must press unrelentingly for quality, integrated education or his whole drive for freedom will be undermined by the absence of a most vital and indispensable element—learning.

"If there is no struggle, there is no progress. Those who profess to favor freedom, and yet depreciate agitation, are men who want crops without plowing up the ground. They want rain without thunder and lightning. They want the ocean without the awful roar of its many waters. This struggle may be a moral one; or it may be a physical one; or it may be both moral and physical; but it must be a struggle. Power concedes nothing without a demand. It never did and it never will." — **Frederick Douglass**

PHOTOGRAPHS DEPICTING IMAGES OF SLAVERY AND THE AFRICAN-AMERICAN EXPERIENCE
(ASSEMBLED FROM VARIOUS US LIBRARY OF CONGRESS COLLECTIONS)

(Library of Congress)

(Library of Congress)

(Library of Congress)

(Library of Congress)

(Library of Congress)

WILSON CHINN, a Branded Slave from Louisiana.
Also exhibiting Instruments of Torture
used to punish Slaves.

Photographed by KIMBALL, 477 Broadway, N.Y

Entered according to Act of Congress, in the year 1863, by
GEO. H. HANKS, in the Clerk's Office of the United States for
the Southern District of New-York.

(Library of Congress)

"Two African American Boys Facing Front" / 1860
(Library of Congress)

"Occupational Portrait if Two African American Chimney Sweeps" / 1860
(Library of Congress)

"Full Length Portrait of an African American Woman Holding a Basket" / 1864
(Library of Congress)

"Group Portrait, possibly a family, with an African American Woman" / 1860
(Library of Congress)

"Mary Allen Watson, 15, June, 1866"
(Library Of Congress"

(Library of Congress)

"Two African American Boys" / 1860
(Library of Congress)

"Fannie Virginia Casseopia Lawrence, a redeemed slave child, five years of age as she appeared when found in slavery. Redeemed in Virginia by Catharine [i.e., Catherine] S. Lawrence; baptized in Brooklyn, at Plymouth Church by Henry Ward Beecher, May 1863 / photographed by Kellogg Brothers, 279 Main Street, Hartford Conn." (Library Of Congress

"African American Man" / 1864
(Library of Congress)

"Gen. Stewart of the Black Horse Cavalry" / 1863
(Library of Congress)

"Civil War Contraband" 1862
(Library of Congress)

"African American Man and Child" / 1860
(Library of Congress)

LEARNING IS WEALTH.

WILSON, CHARLEY, REBECCA & ROSA,

Slaves from New Orleans.

(Library of Congress)

Redeemed in Virginia

By Catharine S. Lawrence. Baptized in Brooklyn, at Plymouth Church, by Henry Ward Beecher, May, 1863. Fannie Virginia Casseopia Lawrence, a Redeemed SLAVE CHILD, 5 years of age.

Entered according to Act of Congress, in the year 1863, by C. S. Lawrence, in the Clerk's Office of the district Court of the United States, for the Southern District of New York.

Photograph by Renowden, 65 Fulton Av. Brooklyn.

(Library of Congress)

Fannie Virginia Casseopia Lawrence.

A redeemed Slave Child, 5 years of age. Redeemed in Virginia, by Catherine S. Lawrence, baptized in Brooklyn, at Plymouth Church, by Henry Ward Beecher, May, 1863.

Entered according to Act of Congress, in the year 1863, by C. S. Lawrence, in the Clerk's office of the District Court of the United States, for the Southern District of New York.

(Library of Congress)

OUR PROTECTION.

ROSA, CHARLEY, REBECCA.

Slave Children from New Orleans.

(Library of Congress)

(Library of Congress)

(Library of Congress)

Sojourner Truth / 1864
(Library of Congress)

"Emancipation" 1863
(Library of Congress)

End

ABOUT THE AUTHOR

Isaias Gamboa is an Afro-Costa Rican-American music producer, songwriter, musician, arranger, author and filmmaker. Born in San Jose, Costa Rica to parents of Spanish and Afro-Caribbean ancestry. His mother, Carmen Gamboa Beckles, was born in the coastal Costa Rican city of Puerto Limon and his father; Danilo Gamboa Mora, from the interior province of San Ramón, Costa Rica.

A music industry veteran, Gamboa has written, performed, produced and arranged more than 200 songs for recording artists including, Shalamar, Gladys Knight & the Pips, Tavares, The Brothers Johnson, Dynasty, The Pointer Sisters and five albums for Rock and Roll Hall of Fame recording artists The Temptations. In 1994 he produced the remix of "Pain" by the late, Tupac Shakur for the Multi-Platinum, Above The Rim soundtrack.

Isaias grew up during the turbulent 1960's and 70's in the primarily African American community of West Adams, Los Angeles. He was first introduced to piano by his mother at age 5 and by age 11, was accomplished in several musical instruments. By age 12 he was playing "Honkey-Tonk" guitar and a particular style of West Coast blues called, Jump blues.

At the age of 13 he was asked to accompany Los Angeles-based Blues singer, Ernie Andrews on the blues guitar; having been schooled in the genre by noted Jump blues guitarist, Edgar Rice of the Alexander Nelson Trio. At age 17, Isaias was discovered by hit R&B producer, Leon Sylvers III, who mentored him over the next 15 years. While still in his teens, he was signed by legendary music industry executive, Clive Davis as a member of the 1980s R&B band, Real To Reel (Arista Records). Notably, after having met Sylvers at a celebrity basketball game in Los Angeles, now-five-time Grammy Award winning music producers, Jimmy Jam and Terry Lewis produced their first ever recordings as professional music producers, "Can You Treat Me Like She Does"[4] and "Don't Keep Me Hangin' On" for Gamboa's band, Real To Reel". Isaias Gamboa was also a founding member of the 1990s neoclassical R&B singing group, "Double Action Theatre" (Polydor Records).

In the 1990s, Gamboa was discovered by legendary music producer, Richard Perry, who mentored him and with whom he would become close friends. Gamboa and Perry worked closely with artists such as, The Pointer Sisters and, The Temptations. In June 2010, Gamboa released a solo CD entitled, "Don't Lie To Me". The CD was released on Gamboa's own label and, featuring his own vocal and instrumental performances, the 12 song collection was also written, produced, performed and arranged by himself. The CD includes performances by famed guitarist, Larry Carlton, The Temptations, drummer, Trevor Lawrence Jr.; singer, Vida Jafari and saxophonist, Donald Hayes.

Isaias Gamboa is a licensed Christian minister with a diverse religious heritage. His mother was Baptist, and his father - Catholic. He also identifies his Jewish heritage through his Jamaican maternal grandmother, Louise Teitelbaum. This background, along with his musical expertise has inspired and informed several important projects in his life. Notable among them is his 2012 book, *We Shall Overcome: Sacred Song On The Devil's Tongue*. Published in 2012, the book is the biography of Louise Shropshire (1913-1993). Shropshire--a hymn writer, civil rights activist and close friend of the Reverend Doctor Martin Luther King Jr., Rev. Fred Shuttlesworth and Rev. Thomas A. Dorsey, played an important role in the creation of the iconic freedom song, "We Shall Overcome."

We Shall Overcome, popularized by Pete Seeger and others, has been credited to "Unknown" for more than half a century, however newly uncovered facts presented in Gamboa's book trace Shropshire's un-credited involvement with the freedom standard to her hymn, "If My Jesus Wills", more commonly known as "I'll Overcome", from which *prima facie* and other evidence indicates "We Shall Overcome" was derived. Gamboa's book was featured at the Author's Pavilion at the 2015 NAACP National Convention.

An abridged and dramatized audio book version of the book, also named, We Shall Overcome: Sacred Song On The Devil's Tongue, was released on Gamboa's label, Plum Recordings in 2011. Narrated and produced by, Gamboa, the four-CD collection also features slave narratives and negro spirituals. A documentary film regarding this subject, written and directed by Isaias Gamboa is scheduled to be completed by fall 2017.

Isaias Gamboa is also the founder of the non-profit organization, We Shall Overcome Foundation. - A Non Profit organization dedicated to the spiritual, physical, social, educational and economic survival and prosperity of poor, ignorant and marginalized people all over the world. On April 12, 2016, the We Shall Overcome Foundation filed a class-action lawsuit in the US District Court for the Southern District of New York against, The Richmond Organization (TRO) and Ludlow Music, Inc., who claim right to the historic anthem. The suit seeks to have the song placed in the public domain, the copyright status of the song revoked and all royalties collected by the companies from its usage, returned. The foundation, which was in the post production process of a feature-length documentary of the song and its history, was refused permission from TRO-Ludlow to use the song.